MAN DOES, WOMAN IS

1964

By Robert Graves

GOOD-BYE TO ALL THAT

THE REAL DAVID COPPERFIELD

I, CLAUDIUS

CLAUDIUS THE GOD

THE ANTIGUA STAMP (ANTIGUA, PENNY, PUCE)

COUNT BELISARIUS

ALMOST FORGOTTEN GERMANY, *translation from the German*

SERGEANT LAMB'S AMERICA (SERGEANT LAMB OF THE NINTH)

With Alan Hodge: THE READER OVER YOUR SHOULDER: A HANDBOOK FOR
   WRITERS OF ENGLISH PROSE

PROCEED, SERGEANT LAMB

With Alan Hodge: THE LONG WEEK-END: A SOCIAL HISTORY OF BRITAIN,
   1919–39

WIFE TO MR. MILTON

KING JESUS

HERCULES, MY SHIPMATE (THE GOLDEN FLEECE)

THE WHITE GODDESS: A HISTORICAL GRAMMAR OF POETIC MYTH

THE COMMON ASPHODEL: COLLECTED ESSAYS ON POETRY, 1922–49

THE ISLANDS OF UNWISDOM

WATCH THE NORTH WIND RISE (SEVEN DAYS IN NEW CRETE)

THE GOLDEN ASS, *translation from the Latin*

OCCUPATION: WRITER

With Joshua Podro: THE NAZARENE GOSPEL RESTORED

ROBERT GRAVES

MAN DOES,
WOMAN IS

1964

Doubleday & Company, Inc.
Garden City, New York

ACKNOWLEDGMENTS

Thanks are due to the following periodicals in whose pages some of these poems have appeared: *The Atlantic Monthly, Georgia Review, Good Housekeeping, Harper's Bazaar, Kenyon Review, McCall's, New Republic, Poetry, Redbook, Saturday Review, Show, Virginia Quarterly Review;* also *Critical Quarterly, The Listener, New Statesman, The Queen, Sunday Times, Times Literary Supplement.* The following poem appeared originally in *The New Yorker:* "The Last Poem."

FOREWORD

Man Does, Woman Is closes a three-book sequence dramatizing the vicissitudes of poetic love. Because such love walks on a knife-edge between two different fates, Parts XV and XVI—these numbers stand for additions to my *Collected Poems*, 1959, and to the 1961 and 1962 supplements—supply alternative endings to the sequence. Part XVII contains miscellaneous poems mostly written under less emotional tension.

R. G.

Deyá,
Majorca.

CONTENTS

XVI

XVII

A TIME OF WAITING

The moment comes when my sound senses
Warn me to keep the pot at a quiet simmer,
Conclude no rash decisions, enter into
No random friendships, check the runaway tongue
And fix my mind in a close caul of doubt—
Which is more difficult, maybe, than to face
Night-long assaults of lurking furies.

The pool lies almost empty; I watch it nursed
By a thin stream. Such idle intervals
Are from waning moon to the new—a moon always
Holds the cords of my heart. Then patience, hands;
Dabble your nerveless fingers in the shallows;
A time shall come when she has need of them.

EXPECT NOTHING

Give, ask for nothing, hope for nothing,
Subsist on crumbs, though scattered casually
Not for you (she smiles) but for the birds.
Though only a thief's diet, it staves off
Dire starvation, nor does she grow fat
On the bread she crumbles, while the lonely truth
Of love is honoured, and her word pledged.

NO LETTER

Be angry yourself, as well you may,
But why with her? She is no party to
Those avaricious dreams that pester you.
Why knot your fists as though plotting to slay
Even our postman George (whose only due
Is a small Christmas box on Christmas Day)
If his delivery does not raise the curse
Of doubt from your impoverished universe?

THE WHY OF THE WEATHER

Since no one knows the why of the weather
Or can authoritatively forecast
More than twelve hours of day or night, at most,
Every poor fool is licenced to explain it
As Heaven's considered judgement on mankind,
And I to account for its vagaries, Myrto,
By inklings of your unaccountable mind.

IN TIME

In time all undertakings are made good,
All cruelties remedied,
Each bond resealed more firmly than before—
Befriend us, Time, Love's gaunt executor!

FIRE WALKER

To be near her is to be near the furnace.
Fortunate boy who could slip idly through,
Basket in hand, culling the red-gold blossom,
Then wander on, untaught that flowers were flame,
With no least smell of scorching on his clothes!
I, at a greater distance, charred to coal,
Earn her reproach for my temerity.

DEED OF GIFT

After close, unembittered meditation
   She gave herself to herself, this time for good;
   Body and heart re-echoed gratitude
For such a merciful repudiation
   Of debts claimed from them by the neighbourhood—

Not only friends, and friends of friends, but lovers
   Whom in the circumstances few could blame
   (Her beauty having singed them like a flame)
If they had hoarded under legal covers
   Old promissory notes signed with her name.

And though to stand once more on the firm road
   From which by misadventure she had strayed,
   So that her journey was that much delayed,
Justified the default of duties owed,
   What debt of true love did she leave unpaid?

AT BEST, POETS

Woman with her forests, moons, flowers, waters,
And watchful fingers:
We claim no magic comparable to hers—
At best, poets; at worst, sorcerers.

SHE IS NO LIAR

She is no liar, yet she will wash away
Honey from her lips, blood from her shadowy hand,
And, dressed at dawn in clean white robes will say,
Trusting the ignorant world to understand:
'Such things no longer are; this is today.'

A LAST POEM

A last poem, and a very last, and yet another—
O, when can I give over?
Must I drive the pen until blood bursts from my nails
And my breath fails and I shake with fever,
Or sit well wrapped in a many-coloured cloak
Where the moon shines new through Castle Crystal?
Shall I never hear her whisper softly:
'But this is truth written by you only,
And for me only; therefore, love, have done'?

anger at some trifle,
nding out
e intrusive grit,
me with perversity
wn torn guts
esultant
strings for her neck?
ut could she swear
corrigible?

THE LEAP

Forget the rest: my heart is true
And in its waking thought of you
Gives the same wild and sudden leap
That jerks it from the brink of sleep.

BANK ACCOUNT

Never again remind me of it:
There are no debts between us.
Though silences, half-promises, evasions
Curb my impatient spirit
And freeze the regular currency of love,
They do not weaken credit. Must I demand
Sworn attestations of collateral,
Forgetting how you looked when first you opened
Our joint account at the Bank of Fate?

JUDGEMENT OF PARIS

What if Prince Paris, after taking thought,
Had not adjudged the apple to Aphrodite
But, instead, had favoured buxom Hera,
Divine defendress of the marriage couch?
What if Queen Helen had been left to squander
Her beauty upon the thralls of Menelaus,
Hector to die unhonoured in his bed,
Penthesileia to hunt a poorer quarry,
The bards to celebrate a meaner siege?
Could we still have found the courage, you and I,
To embark together for Cranaë
And consummate our no less fateful love?

MAN DOES, WOMAN IS

Studiously by lamplight I appraised
The palm of your hand, its heart-line
Identical with its head-line;
And you appraised the approving frown.

I spread my cards face-upwards on the table,
Not challenging you for yours.
Man does; but woman is—
Can a gamester argue with his luck?

THE AMPLE GARDEN

However artfully you transformed yourself
Into bitch, vixen, tigress,
I knew the woman behind.

Light as a bird now, you descend at dawn
From the poplar bough or ivy bunch
To peck my strawberries,

And have need indeed of an ample garden:
All my fruits, fountains, arbours, lawns
In fief to your glory.

You, most unmetaphorically you:
Call me a Catholic, so devout in faith
I joke of love, as Catholics do of God,
And scorn all exegesis.

TO MYRTO ABOUT HERSELF

Fierce though your love of her may be,
    What man alive can doubt
I love her more? Come now, agree
Not to turn rivalrous of me,
    Lest you and I fall out!

And should her law make little sense
    Even at times to you,
Love has its own sure recompense:
To love beyond all reason—hence
    Her fondness for us two.

What she pursues we neither know
    Nor can we well inquire;
But if you carelessly bestow
A look on me she did not owe
    It comes at her desire.

THE THREE-FACED

Who calls her two-faced? Faces, she has three:
The first inscrutable, for the outer world;
The second shrouded in self-contemplation;
The third, her face of love,
Once for an endless moment turned on me.

DAZZLE OF DARKNESS

The flame guttered, flared impossibly high,
Went out for good; yet in the dazzle of darkness
I saw her face ashine like an angel's:
Beauty too memorable for lamentation,
Though doomed to rat and maggot.

MYRRHINA

O, why judge Myrrhina
As though she were a man?
She obeys a dark wisdom
(As Eve did before her)
Which never can fail,
Being bound by no pride
Of armorial bearings
Bequeathed in tail male.

And though your blood brother
Who dared to do you wrong
In his greed of Myrrhina
Might plead a like wisdom
The fault to excuse,
Myrrhina is just:
She has hanged the poor rogue
By the neck from her noose.

FOOD OF THE DEAD

Blush as you stroke the curves—chin, lips and brow—
Of your scarred face, Prince Orpheus: for she has called it
Beautiful, nor would she stoop to flattery.
Yet are you patient still, when again she has eaten
Food of the dead, seven red pomegranate seeds,
And once more warmed the serpent at her thighs
For a new progress through new wards of hell?

EURYDICE

'I am oppressed, I am oppressed, I am oppressed'—
Once I utter the curse, how can she rest:
No longer able, weeping, to placate me
With renewed auguries of celestial beauty?

Speak, fly in her amber ring; speak, horse of gold!
What gift did I ever grudge her, or help withhold?
In a mirror I watch blood trickling down the wall—
Is it mine? Yet still I stand here, proud and tall.

Look where she shines with a borrowed blaze of light
Among the cowardly, faceless, lost, unright,
Clasping a naked imp to either breast—
Am I not oppressed, oppressed, three times oppressed?

She has gnawn at corpse-flesh till her breath stank,
Paired with a jackal, grown distraught and lank,
Crept home, accepted solace, but then again
Flown off to chain truth back with an iron chain.

My own dear heart, dare you so war on me
As to strangle love in a mad perversity?
Is ours a fate can ever be forsworn
Though my lopped head sing to the yet unborn?

TO BEGUILE AND BETRAY

To beguile and betray, though pardonable in women,
Slowly quenches the divine need-fire
By true love kindled in them. Have you not watched
The immanent Goddess fade from their brows
When they make private to her mysteries
Some whip-scarred rogue from the hulks, some painted
                                                    clown
From the pantomime—and afterwards accuse you
Of jealous hankering for the mandalot
Rather than horror and sick foreboding
That she will never return to the same house?

I WILL WRITE

He had done for her all that a man could,
And, some might say, more than a man should,
Then was ever a flame so recklessly blown out
Or a last goodbye so negligent as this?
'I will write to you,' she muttered briefly,
Tilting her cheek for a polite kiss;
Then walked away, nor ever turned about . . .

Long letters written and mailed in her own head—
There are no mails in a city of the dead.

BIRD OF PARADISE

At sunset, only to his true love,
The bird of paradise opened wide his wings
Displaying emerald plumage shot with gold
Unguessed even by him.
                                    True, that wide crest
Had blazoned royal estate, and the tropic flowers
Through which he flew had shown example
Of what brave colours gallantry might flaunt,
But these were other. She asked herself, trembling:
'What did I do to awake such glory?'

THE METAPHOR

The act of love seemed a dead metaphor
For love itself, until the timeless moment
When fingers trembled, heads clouded,
And love rode everywhere, too numinous
To be expressed or greeted calmly:
O, then it was, deep in our own forest,
We dared revivify the metaphor,
Shedding the garments of this epoch
In scorn of time's wilful irrelevancy;
So at last understood true nakedness
And the long debt to silence owed.

SONG: A PHOENIX FLAME

In my heart a phoenix flame
    Darts and scorches me all day—
Should a fierce sun do the same,
    I die away.

O for pools with sunken rocks,
    Minnow-haunted mountain brooks,
Blustering gales of Equinox,
    Cold, green nooks.

Who could boast a careless wit,
    Doubly roasted, heart and hide,
Turning on the Sun's red spit,
    Consumed inside?

SECRECY

Lovers are happy
When favoured by chance,
But here is blessedness
Beyond all happiness,

Not to be gainsaid
By any gust of chance,
Harvest of one vine,
Gold from the same mine:

To keep which sacred
Demands a secrecy
That the word might blame
As deceit and shame;

Yet to publish which
Would make a him and her
Out of me and you
That were both untrue.

Let pigeons couple
Brazonly on the bough,
But royal stag and hind
Are of our own mind.

JOSEPH AND MARY

They turned together with a shocked surprise—
He, old and fabulous; she, young and wise—
Both having heard a newborn hero weep
In convalescence from the stroke of sleep.

AN EAST WIND

Beware the giddy spell, ground fallen away
Under your feet, wings not yet beating steady:
An ignorant East Wind tempts you to deny
Faith in the twofold glory of your being—
You with a thousand leagues or more to fly.

'Poised in air between earth and paradise,
Paradise and earth, confess which pull
Do you find the stronger? Is it of homesickness
Or of passion? Would you be rather loyal or wise?
How are these choices reconcilable?'

Turn from him without anger. East Wind knows
Only one wall of every foursquare house,
Has never viewed your northern paradise
Nor watched its queen tending her jewelled boughs,
But always from the same sick quarter blows.

DANCE OF WORDS

To make them move, you should start from lightning
And not forecast the rhythm: rely on chance,
Or so-called chance, for its bright emergence
Once lightning interpenetrates the dance.

Grant them their own traditional steps and postures
But see they dance it out again and again
Until only lightning is left to puzzle over—
The choreography plain, and the theme plain.

A BLIND ARROW

Though your blind arrow, shot in time of need
Among the shadowy birches, did indeed
Strike, as you knew it must, the assassin's heart,
Never disparage a trained bowman's art.

THE OLEASTER

Each night for seven nights beyond the gulf
A storm raged, out of hearing, and crooked flashes
Of lightning animated us. Before day-break
Rain fell munificently for the earth's need . . .

No, here they never plant the sweet olive
As some do (bedding slips in a prepared trench),
But graft it on the club of Hercules
The savage, inexpugnable oleaster
Whose roots and bole bunching from limestone crannies
Sprout impudent shoots born only to be lopped
Spring after Spring. Theirs is a loveless berry . . .

By mid-day we walk out, with naked feet,
Through pools on the road, gazing at waterfalls
Or a line of surf, but mostly at the trees
Whose elegant branches rain has duly blackened
And pressed their crowns to a sparkling silver.

Innumerable, plump with promise of oil,
The olives hang grass-green, in thankfulness
For a bitter sap and bitter New Year snows
That cleansed their bark . . .
                                    Forgive me, dearest love,
If nothing I can say be strange or new.
I am no child of the hot South like you,
Though in rock rooted like an oleaster.

THE SEPTUAGENARIAN

Youth is the ruggedest burden that can score
Your septuagenarian shoulder:
If you should threaten, as before, to powder
Rocks with bare heels, or rend the oak asunder
With naked fingers, you can now no more
Plead youthful benefit of metaphor.
Such unsubstantiated boasts will be
Substantial evidence of senility.

NON COGUNT ASTRA

Come, live in Now and occupy it well.
Prediction's no alternative to forethought
Despite at least four hundred arts of scrying
The dubious future, such as to study birds,
Or bull's guts, or sheep droppings, or wine lees
In an alabaster cup. True, the most ancient
Most exact discipline, astrology,
Comes hallowed by a college of gowned mantics
Who still cast horoscopes only by stars
Apparent to the still unaided eye—
And of whom a few, the best, focus their powers
On exact horary configurations, then
At an agreed moment brusquely sweep away
Zodiacal signs, conjunctions, trines
And reinduce a pure, archaic vision;
Yet disregard all false astrologers
Who dare lay greedy or compulsive hands
On the stars you sped at your nativity
Along their courses and forbad to canker
The rose of love or blunt the blade of honour:
No public hangmen these, but servants chosen
To wear bright livery at your house gate;
And favour you the more, the less you fear them.

SONG: SWORD AND ROSE

The King of Hearts a broadsword bears,
　　The Queen of Hearts, a rose—
Though why, not every gambler cares
　　Or cartomancer knows.

Be beauty yours, be honour mine,
　　Yet sword and rose are one:
Great emblems that in love combine
　　Until the dealing's done;

For no card, whether small or face,
　　Shall overtrump our two
Except that Heart of Hearts, the Ace,
　　To which their title's due.

ENDLESS PAVEMENT

In passage along an endless, eventless pavement,
None but the man in love, as he turns to stare
At the glazed eyes flickering past, will remain aware
Of his own, assured, meticulous, rustic tread—
As if pavement were pebbles, or rocks overgrown by grasses;
And houses, trees with birds flying overhead.

IN DISGUISE

Almost I welcome the dirty subterfuges
Of this unreal world closing us in,
That present you as a lady of high fashion
And me as a soldier on the pensioned list.

Our conversation is infinitely proper,
With a peck on either cheek as we meet or part—
Yet the seven archons of the heavenly stair
Tremble at the disclosure of our seals.

A MEASURE OF CASUALNESS

Too fierce the candlelight; your gentle voice
Roars as in dream; my shoulder-nooks flower;
A scent of honeysuckle invades the house,
And my fingertips are so love-enhanced
That sailcloth feels like satin to them.
Teach me a measure of casualness
Though you stalk into my room like Venus naked.

IN TIME OF ABSENCE

Lovers in time of absence need not signal
With call and answering call:
By sleight of providence each sends the other
A clear, more than coincidental answer
To every still unformulated puzzle,
Or a smile at a joke harboured, not yet made,
Or power to be already wise and unafraid.

THE GREEN CASTLE

The first heaven is a flowery plain;
The second, a glass mountain;
The third, likewise terrestrial,
Is an orchard-close unclouded
By prescience of death or change
Or the blood-sports of desire:
Our childhood paradise.

The next three heavens, known as celestial,
Are awkward of approach.
Mind is the prudent rider; body, the ass
Disciplined always by a harsh bit,
Accepts his daily diet of thorns
And frugal, brackish water;
Holds converse with archangels.

The seventh heaven, most unlike those others,
We once contrived to enter
By a trance of love; it is a green castle
Girdled with ramparts of blue sea
And silent but for the waves' leisured wash.
There Adam rediscovered Eve:
She wrapped him in her arms.

An afterglow of truth, still evident
When we had fallen earthward,
Astonished all except the born blind.
Strangers would halt us in the roadway:
'Confess where you have been.'
And, at a loss, we replied stumblingly:
'It was here, it was nowhere—
Last night we lodged at a green castle,
Its courtyard paved with gold.'

NOT TO SLEEP

Not to sleep all the night long, for pure joy,
Counting no sheep and careless of chimes,
Welcoming the dawn confabulation
Of birds, her children, who discuss idly
Fanciful details of the promised coming—
Will she be wearing red, or russet, or blue,
Or pure white?—whatever she wears, glorious:
Not to sleep all the night long, for pure joy,
This is given to few but at last to me,
So that when I laugh and stretch and leap from bed
I shall glide downstairs, my feet brushing the carpet
In courtesy to civilized progression,
Though, did I wish, I could soar through the open window
And perch on a branch above, acceptable ally
Of the birds still alert, grumbling gently together.

THE HEARTH

Here it begins: the worm of love breeding
Among red embers of a hearth-fire
Turns to a chick, is slowly fledged,
And will hop from lap to lap in a ring
Of eager children basking at the blaze.

But the luckless man who never sat there,
Nor borrowed live coals from the sacred source
To warm a hearth of his own making,
Nor bedded lay under pearl-grey wings
In dutiful content,

How shall he watch at the stroke of midnight
Dove become phoenix, plumed with green and gold?
Or be caught up by jewelled talons
And haled away to a fastness of the hills
Where an unveiled woman, black as Mother Night,
Teaches him a new degree of love
And the tongues and songs of birds?

THAT OTHER WORLD

Fatedly alone with you once more
As before Time first creaked:
Sole woman and sole man.

Others admire us as we walk this world:
We show them kindliness and mercy,
So be it none grow jealous
Of the truth that echoes between us two,
Or of that other world, in the world's cradle,
Child of your love for me.

THE BEDS OF GRAINNE AND DIARMUID

How many secret nooks in copse or glen
We sained for ever with our pure embraces,
No man shall know; though indeed master poets
Reckon one such for every eve of the year,
To sain their calendar.
                     But this much is true:
That children stumbling on our lairs by chance
In quest of hazel-nuts or whortleberries
Will recognize the impress of twin bodies
On the blue-green turf, starred with diversity
Of alien flowers, and shout astonishment.
Yet should some amorous country pair, presuming
To bask in joy on any bed of ours,
Offend against the love by us exampled,
Long ivy roots will writhe up from beneath
And bitterly fetter ankle, wrist and throat.

RAIN OF BRIMSTONE

Yet if they trust by lures or spells
   To exorcise the tall angel,
Love, from this ancient keep by us
   Now long frequented,

And if frustration turns their wits,
   So that they bawl in hell's fury
Battering at our gate all night
   With oaken cudgels,

Are we to blame for sparing them
   The voice of truth which they deny us?
Should we not darkly leave the town
   To its rain of brimstone?

CONSORTIUM OF STONES

The stones you have gathered, of diverse shapes,
Chosen from sea strand, lake strand, mountain gully:
Lay them all out on a basalt slab together
But allow intervals for light and air,
These being human souls; and reject any
With crumpled calceous edges and no feature
That awakes loving correspondence.

Start at this pair: blue flint, grey ironstone,
Which you ring around with close affinities
In every changeless colour, hatched, patched, plain—
Curve always answering curve; and angle, angle.

Gaps there may be, which next year or the next
Will fill to a marvel: never jog Time's arm,
Only narrow your eyes when you walk about
Lest they miss what is missing. The agreed intent
Of each consortium, whether of seven stones,
Or of nineteen, or thirty-three, or more,
Must be a circle, with firm edges outward,
Each various element aware of the sum.

THE BLACK GODDESS

Silence, words into foolishness fading,
Silence prolonged, of thought so secret
We hush the sheep-bells and the loud cicada.

And your black agate eyes, wide open, mirror
The released firebird beating his way
Down a whirled avenue of blues and yellows.

Should I not weep? Profuse the berries of love,
The speckled fish, the filberts and white ivy
Which you, with a half-smile, bestow
On your delectable broad land of promise
For me, who never before went gay in plumes.

BROKEN NECK

'Some forty years ago or maybe more,'
Pronounced the radiologist, 'you broke
Your neck: that is to say, contrived to fracture
Your sixth cervical vertebra—see here,
The picture's clear—and between sixth and seventh
Flattened this cartilage to uselessness:
Hence rheumatism. Surely you recall
Some incident? We all do foolish things
While young, and obstinately laugh them off—
Till they catch up with us in God's good time.
Let me prescribe you a Swiss analgesic
Which should at least . . .'
                      Love, I still laugh it off
And all Swiss mercenary alleviations,
For though I broke my neck in God's good time
It is in yours alone I choose to live.

O

'*O per se O, O per se O!*',
The moribund grammarian cried
To certain scholars grouped at his bedside,
Spying the round, dark pit a-gape below:
'*O per se O!*'

WOMAN OF GREECE

By your knees they rightly clasp you,
   Strong sons of your bed,
Whom you get, kneeling; and bear, kneeling;
   Kneeling, mourn for dead.

THE COLOURS OF NIGHT

The Moon never makes use of the Sun's palette.
Admire her silvery landscapes, but abstain
From record of them: lest you be later tempted
To counterfeit the dangerous colours of Night
Which are man's blood spurted on moving cloud.

BETWEEN TRAINS

Arguing over coffee at the station,
Neither of us noticed her dark beauty,
Though she sat close by, until suddenly
Three casual words—does it matter what they were?—
Spoken without remarkable intonation
Or accent, so bewildered him and me,
As it were catching the breath of our conversation,
That each set down his coffee-cup, to stare.
'You have come for us?' my lips cautiously framed—
Her eyes were almost brighter than I could bear—
But she rose and left, unready to be named.

TO THE TEUMESSIAN VIXEN

Do not mistake me: I was never a rival
  Of that poor fox who pledged himself to win
Your heart by gnawing away his brush. Who ever
  Proved love was love except by a whole skin?

THE HUNG WU VASE

With women like Marie no holds are barred.
Where do they get the gall? How can they do it?

She stormed out, slamming the hall door so hard
That a vase on the gilt shelf above—you knew it,
Loot from the Summer Palace at Pekin
And worth the entire contents of my flat—
Toppled and fell . . .
                I poured myself straight gin,
Downing it at a gulp. 'So that was that!'

The bell once more . . . Marie walked calmly in,
Observed broken red porcelain on the mat,
Looked up, looked down again with condescension,
Then, gliding past me to retrieve a glove
(Her poor excuse for this improper call),
Muttered: 'And one thing I forget to mention:
Your Hung Wu vase was phoney, like your love!'

How can they do it? Where do they get the gall?

LA MEJICANA

Perfect beneath an eight-rayed sun you lie,
    Rejoiced at his caresses. Yours is a land
For pumas, chillis, and men dark of eye;
    Yet summon me with no derisive hand
From these remote moon-pastures drenched in dew—
And watch who burns the blacker: I or you.

LAMIA IN LOVE

Need of this man was her ignoble secret:
Desperate for love, yet loathing to deserve it,
She wept pure tears of sorrow when his eyes
Betrayed mistrust in her impeccable lies.

AFTER THE FLOOD

Noah retrieves the dove again,
  Which bears him in its bill
A twig of olive to explain
That, if God sends them no more rain,
  The world may prosper still.

Shem, Ham and Japheth raise a shout,
  But weeks on end must wait
Till Father Noah, venturing out,
Can view the landscape all about
  And prophesy their fate.

'Where have the waters of God's Flood
  Dispersed?' God only knew.
What Noah saw was miles of mud,
Drowned rogues, and almond trees in bud
  With blossom peeping through.

'Bold lads, in patience here abide!
  This mire around the ark
By wind or sun must well be dried
Before we set against her side
  The planks to disembark.'

Obedient sons, a virtuous wife,
  Flocks, cattle, jars of seeds,
Crook, coulter, halter, pruning-knife—
Noah forecasts a brave new life
  Agreeable to his needs.

Exult with him at the clear sky,
  Proud Noahs of today,
For though we here and there descry
Morasses that no sun can dry
  (Regret them how we may),

God's rainbow is a glorious toy,
  His wine a cheerful drink,
And since He chooses to destroy
Folk better dead, we wish Him joy,
  While choking at the stink.

A LATE ARRIVAL

A Libyan pilgrim-ship tied up at Joppa
Twenty-four hours late, on a Wednesday morning.
The poor Jew from Cyrene hired no ass
But trudged, by way of Gimzo and Beth Horon,
Three hundred stadia to Jerusalem.

That Friday morning, close to the Western Gate
Where his son Alexander welcomed him,
He was tapped on the wrist by a Roman sergeant
And, though with little on his conscience, jumped
In excusable fright. The grinning sergeant said:
'A work of charity awaits you, sir!'

Foot-sore Simon, thus impressed to shoulder
The eight-foot oaken cross-piece of a cross
Towards Jeremiah's grotto—now already
Late for a family gathering and, far worse,
Contaminated by this unclean baulk—
Vented his rage on the condemned bandit:

'Poor fool! Betrayed to those Boethan traitors
By one of your own men, my son reports!
How long had you known Judah of Cherioth?
Seven years, or more? Alas, what innocence!
So long, and never peered into his heart?
I heard him once, far too loud in your praise
(Three Passovers ago, it must have been),
And all but naming you the Appointed King . . .
I am told that Judah, jealous for your honour

Yet jealous of you, boasting he knew best,
Pleaded for your protective custody;
Loved you, he said, but loved our nation more.'

Since the poor stumbling felon made no answer,
Though his lips moved, as it might be in prayer,
Simon thought pityingly of Alexander:
What a disgrace for his own son to see him
Hauled off to attend a Roman crucifixion!
Why had God's hand delayed that Libyan ship?

Later the man spoke in a small, dry voice:
'May God forgive me and my servant too—
We both thought we knew better than our lord.'

SONG: WITH NO RETURN

If you keep your heart so true
    That her oaks take fire and burn,
And her foxes dance for you
All together in full view,
    Paradise is here to earn,
    Peace to learn:
She will pledge you, as she must,
To a trust beyond all trust
    With no manner of return.

ALL I TELL YOU FROM MY HEART

I begged my love to wait a bit
    Although the sky was clear:
'I smell a shower of rain,' said I,
    'And you'll be caught, I fear.'
'You want to keep me trapped,' she said,
    'And hold my hand again . . .'
But not ten minutes had she gone
    When how the rain did rain!

'Alas, dear love, so wet you are—
    You should have trusted me!
For all I tell you from my heart
    Is sure as prophecy.'

I begged my love to wait a bit
    And watch the faggots blaze.
'There's a music on the march,' said I,
    'To cheer whoever stays.'
'You want to keep me trapped,' she said,
    'O, every night's the same . . .'
But not ten minutes had she gone
    When in the fiddlers came!

'Alas, dear love, what tunes they played—
    You should have trusted me!
For all I tell you from my heart
    Is sure as prophecy.'

I begged my love to take good heed
　　When walking through the wood,
And warned her of a random rogue
　　Who brought the world no good.
'You want to keep me trapped,' she said,
　　'And roll me in your bed . . .'
But scarce a hundred yards from home
　　She lost her maidenhead.

'Alas, dear love, it is too late—
　　You should have trusted me!
For all I told you from my heart
　　Was sure as prophecy.'

THE UNDEAD

To be the only woman alive in a vast hive of death
Is a strange predicament, granted! Innumerable zombies
With glazed eyes shuffle around at their diurnal tasks,
Keep the machines whirring, drudge idly in stores and bars,
Bear still-born zombie children, pack them off to school
For education in science and the dead languages,
Divert themselves with moribund travesties of living,
Lay mountainous bets on horses never seen to run,
Speed along highways in conveyor-belt automobiles
But, significantly enough, often dare overshoot
The traffic signals and *boing!* destroy themselves again,
Earning expensive funerals. (These, if at last they emerge
From the select green cemetery plots awarded them
On their twenty-first death-days by sombre uncles and aunts,
Will become zombies of the second degree, reverenced
Nationwide in church or synagogue.)
                                        Nevertheless,
Let none of this daunt you, child! Accept it as your fate
To live, to love, knowingly to cause true miracles,
Nor ever to find your body possessed by a cold corpse.
For one day, as you choose an unfamiliar side-street
Keeping both eyes open, alert, not apprehensive,
You shall suddenly (this is a promise) come to a brief halt:
For striding towards you on the same sidewalk will appear
A young man with the halo of life around his head,
Will catch you reassuringly by both hands, asseverating
In phrases utterly unintelligible to a zombie
That all is well: you are neither diseased, deranged, nor
                                        mistaken

But merely undead. He will name others like you, no less
                                                    alive:
Two girls and a man, all moneyless immigrants arrived
Lately at a new necropolitan conurbation.
'Come with me, girl, and join them! The dead, you will
                                                  observe,
Can exercise no direct sanctions against the living
And therefore doggedly try to omit them from all the records.
Still, they cannot avoid a certain morbid fascination
With what they call our genius. They will venture questions
But never wait for an answer—being doubtless afraid
That it will make their ears burn, or their eyes prick with
                                                   tears—
Nor can they countermand what orders we may issue.'

Nod your assent, go with him, do not even return to pack!
When five live people room together, each rates as a
                                                  million—
But encourage the zombies to serve you, the honest
                                                 creatures,
For though one cannot ameliorate their way of death
By telling them true stories or singing them real songs,
They will feel obscurely honoured by your warm presence.